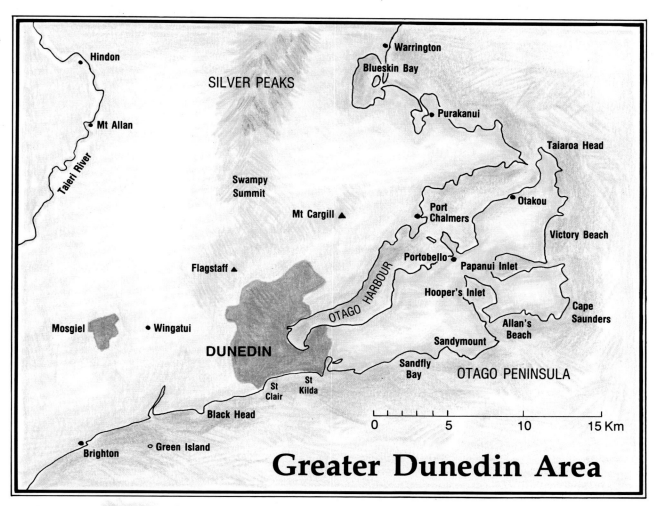

Greater Dunedin Area

Labels: Hindon, Warrington, Blueskin Bay, SILVER PEAKS, Mt Allan, Purakanui, Taieri River, Taiaroa Head, Swampy Summit, Port Chalmers, Otakou, Mt Cargill, Victory Beach, Flagstaff, Portobello, Papanui Inlet, OTAGO HARBOUR, Hooper's Inlet, Cape Saunders, Mosgiel, Wingatui, Allan's Beach, Sandymount, DUNEDIN, Sandfly Bay, OTAGO PENINSULA, St Clair, St Kilda, Black Head, Brighton, Green Island

0 5 10 15 Km

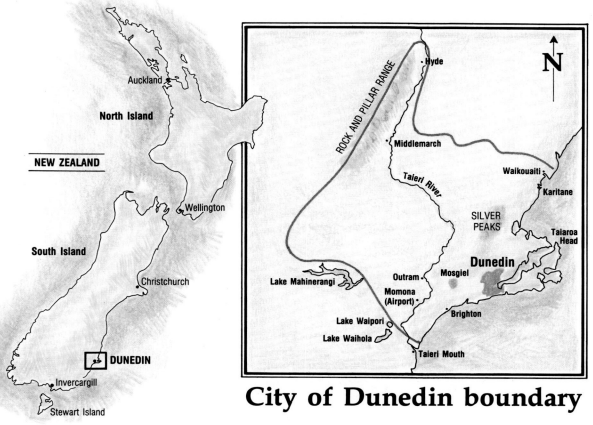

New Zealand inset: Auckland, North Island, NEW ZEALAND, Wellington, South Island, Christchurch, DUNEDIN, Invercargill, Stewart Island

City of Dunedin boundary inset: ROCK AND PILLAR RANGE, Hyde, Middlemarch, Taieri River, Waikouaiti, Karitane, SILVER PEAKS, Taiaroa Head, Dunedin, Lake Mahinerangi, Outram, Mosgiel, Momona (Airport), Brighton, Lake Waipori, Lake Waihola, Taieri Mouth

City of Dunedin boundary

Downtown Dunedin has a symmetrical shape, marked out by the Octagon and Moray Place, which lie handy to the wharf area.

DUNEDIN
A PORTRAIT

Neville Peat

ROGER HALL
PETER HAYDEN
LOIS GALER

Hyndman Publishing

ISBN 0-473-02174-9

AUTHOR PROFILES

NEVILLE PEAT

A fifth generation descendant of Scottish settlers in Otago, Neville Peat is an author, journalist and photographer whose 17 titles include guidebooks (to Dunedin and the West Coast) and several books on natural history themes, including the world of albatrosses and penguins. His widely acclaimed book, *The Falcon and the Lark,* is set in the Strath Taieri, the rural outskirts of Dunedin City.

ROGER HALL

A playwright of international standing, Roger Hall teaches in the English Department of the University of Otago. He has written numerous box office hits, some of which have been adapted for television and film. He is patron of the Fortune and Globe Theatres in Dunedin, and he initiated New Zealand Writers' Week, which is held biennially in the city.

PETER HAYDEN

A television personality, Peter Hayden has lived in Dunedin since 1979, when he joined Television New Zealand's Natural History Unit. He has presented, directed or produced numerous documentaries, several of which have won international awards.

LOIS GALER

Lois Galer represents the New Zealand Historic Places Trust in Otago and Southland as its Regional Officer, based in Dunedin. She is the author of five books on the buildings of Dunedin and Otago, and she has taken a leading role in campaigns to save several significant city buildings.

ACKNOWLEDGEMENTS

The publisher and author are grateful for the written contributions of Roger Hall, Peter Hayden and Lois Galer, and for the rights to reproduce photographs by Greg Gordon, Rod Morris, Dean Schneider and Perran Tonkin. All other photographs are by Neville Peat.

Writers quoted in the text are: Alexander Bathgate, Thomas Bracken, Charles Brasch, Lauris Edmond, Denis Glover, Christine Johnston and Hone Tuwhare.

Contents

First published 1993
Hyndman Publishing, P.O. Box 5017, Dunedin, New Zealand
Reprinted 1997, 1999

Book Design and Maps by Jenny Cooper
Printed through Bookprint Consultants, Wellington

PUBLISHER'S NOTE

Neil Hyndman

Superb scenery, spectacular wildlife and a wonderful built heritage together make Dunedin very special. They are the basis of Dunedin's standing as an important tourist destination heading into the 21st century. This portrait of the city is a recognition of those attributes. It complements a set of three companion booklets that have appeared in the past couple of years: *Dunedin, Wild & Scenic Dunedin* and *Heritage Dunedin*. We decided the city deserved an expanded edition that combined a selection of the best photographs from the earlier publications with Neville Peat's newest photographs and written contributions from Dunedin personalities Roger Hall, Peter Hayden and Lois Galer. Over 100 new images are merged with some 30 "best shots" from the earlier titles.

As Neville says in his scene-setting essay, Dunedin people are awakening to the delights of their city, and they are pleased to share these delights with a wide cross-section of visitors from overseas and other parts of New Zealand. We trust this book enhances that new awareness of Dunedin's outstanding appeal.

Brighton is a popular seaside township to the south of the city, where rock outcrops add interest to the sandy shores. The township is built around a small river.

Foreword

ROGER HALL

The first time I drove up Dunedin's High Street, my heart soared with the road, exhilarated by the architecture, the oldness of everything, the feel of the place. I was to be here for a year, and High Street provided a wonderful entrance to what lay ahead. Sixteen years later I am still here for, like so many of the University's Burns Fellows — and Mozart and Hodgkins Fellows (music and art) — I have stayed on to make the place my home.

Why? Dunedin is a nice size; most things are at walking distance. You can get a parking space, and the rush hour lasts for 20 minutes at most. Dunedin believes in education — the schools are all good — and it is the only true university city in the country, thanks to students being able to live almost on or close to the campus. The city has a centre and a heart, and a shopping area that retains the old sense of being downtown.

But most of all, Dunedin is a continual delight to the eye. You can drive directly through it (on the one-way system), but you can't drive directly across. Round every corner there are curves, hills and valleys, gullies, cliffs, steps, paths, high hedges, splendid gardens. The harbour is glimpsed or suddenly spread out before you. Best of all are the buildings: villas and mansions, cottages or huge Gothic institutions, terrace rows and churches with spires that pierce the sky. Wood, brick, concrete, stone; they're all here, many with roofs that delight. Look up, too, for the attics, the towers, the turrets. The variations in the slate roofs are worth a tour of their own.

When other New Zealand cities were pulling down their oldest and finest buildings, Dunedin left most of hers right where they were. The result is a fine Victorian city which its citizens and, more recently, its city council have come to appreciate more and more. The Council's restoration of the Octagon and Municipal Chambers justly won a major architectural award.

Perhaps the least appreciated treasures are the big old wooden houses, many of which are being painted in bright colours, reminiscent of San Francisco's "Painted Ladies" (I admit to a vested interest; I live in one and we recently painted it in bright colours).

If the city is a continual delight to the eye, then so is the Peninsula. I always take visitors along Highcliff for them to revel in the views of the harbour on our way out to the albatrosses. On the Peninsula it feels as though the clock has been set back 40 years — instant nostalgia for the way we were. And one other visit never fails to impress — Tunnel Beach.

Don't stay too long in Dunedin — you may never leave.

The Municipal Chambers in the Octagon, handsome on a warm spring morning.

Snow tussock and mountain flax decorate the brow of Flagstaff, the city's subalpine backdrop.

An Unfolding Panorama

NEVILLE PEAT

Dunedin's roles are many. A university town; New Zealand's southernmost main centre; commercial hub of Otago (and the nation last century); wildlife capital; refuge for old and graceful architecture. More than any other New Zealand city, Dunedin embraces its built, historic heritage and its natural heritage with equal enthusiasm, beckoning visitors with both. What eventuates is a variety show. The images range from stone spires and turrets to snow tussock, saltmarsh and shining sand, and from Gothic archways to gliding albatrosses.

> "I grew to know most of the country around Dunedin, in all its variousness. It impressed itself upon me so strongly that it seemed to accompany me always."
>
> **Charles Brasch**
> **"Indirections: A Memoir" 1980**

From encircling hills, an amphitheatre of sorts, the city tends to face the harbour rather than the sea as if the sea were too much to fathom and less comfortable to live with than a long, sinuous harbour no wider than a large river in places. In 1844, four years before Dunedin was established as the Chief Town of the Otago Settlement, surveyor Frederick Tuckett described this setting as "an ornamental and commodious site for a town, most suitable in every way". Anyone who approaches Dunedin by road from the north would have to agree. From the motorway a panorama unfolds of hills and valleys descending to harbour and sea. The flat land surrounding the head of the harbour holds the city centre and binds Otago Peninsula to the mainland. It is an inviting vista.

The setting, however pleasant now, had fiery origins. The city occupies an eroded and long dormant volcano. Between 10 and 13 million years ago a series of volcanic eruptions built up a mountainous knuckle on the Otago coastline. Over eons, river erosion along a fault line dissected this great knuckle and the sea filled the resulting trough. Thus Otago Harbour was formed (photo, **pages 16-17**). Mount Cargill, 680

metres, and adjacent peaks overlooking the harbour are monuments to the mountain-building power of the volcano. Old lava flows form many a headland on Otago Peninsula, and the strange interlocking columns of basalt rock that are featured at such places as the Organ Pipes, the Pyramids and Black Head provide graphic evidence of the cooling process.

Tunnel Beach, a spectacular piece of coastline, offers a glimpse of the geology of Dunedin before the volcano changed the landscape forever. Here the cliffs and islets, untouched by lava flows, are composed of a creamy sandstone, weathered into curious shapes by wave, wind and rain.

As a result of local government reorganisation in 1989, the boundaries of the City of Dunedin now extend over an hour's drive inland to the Rock and Pillar Range at the eastern edge of Central Otago. No longer is Dunedin simply the hills and flat land surrounding Otago Harbour, although most people recognise the city proper as the built-up areas below the brooding, burly backdrop of Flagstaff and Mount Cargill. The enlarged Dunedin, however, is a diverse place spanning schist rock landscapes (as at Sutton and the Silver Peaks Range), the middle reaches of the Taieri River, the impressive Taieri Gorge and intensively farmed Taieri Plain, and the estuaries of Waikouaiti, Blueskin Bay and Purakanui.

All up, the land area of Dunedin is 3350 square kilometres, much of it zoned rural and

A winter's day at Pukehiki, Otago Peninsula.

sparsely populated. Dunedin's population is about 118,000, over two-thirds of whom (about 80,000) live within the circle of volcanic hills, the city's heart. Here, one in five citizens is a student of one of the three big tertiary institutions – University of Otago, Otago Polytechnic and College of Education. Their campuses form a precinct north of the city centre, and the bulk of their student populations, from other parts of New Zealand or overseas, live in rented houses and hostels nearby. Education is the city's leading industry, and its biggest employer. The students are more than economic indicators, however. They add verve and conviviality to the city's social fabric.

Education has always figured prominently in local history. From the outset in 1848, Dunedin's Scottish founders made education a priority. Dunedin boasted the country's first university and first teachers' college. Specialised education was catered for later in schools of medicine, dentistry, mining, physical education and physiotherapy. Dunedin and higher learning became synonymous.

In the planning stages the new settlement was known as "New Edinburgh" after the Scottish capital. When it was pointed out that too many places in North America had been called "New" this and "New" that, the Otago settlement's Chief Town was renamed Dunedin – the ancient Celtic name for Edinburgh, a name that had been in poetic use for centuries. Thus the link was maintained with the old country.

To reinforce that link, the town planners applied Edinburgh street and suburban names aplenty. Among the street names carried halfway round the world were George and Princes (each end of the main street, divided by the Octagon), High, Castle and St Andrew. At the centre of development was the Octagon, encircled by Moray Place.

"The severe spire of Knox Church in George Street, the Gothic archways of the university and the old-fashioned stylishness of many of the public buildings combined with the thin cold Leith and its stone bridges to shed an atmosphere of dignity and permanence.

Lauris Edmond
"Bonfires in the Rain" 1991

To their credit, the planners added a green belt – a 240ha corridor of evergreen native forest curving through the town's "dress circle" of hill suburbs. Exotic deciduous trees were interplanted through the Town Belt, decorating it with red, brown and yellow hues in autumn – an arresting sight now that the trees have grown tall.

When the first European settlers arrived, native forest reached the water's edge along much of the harbour. Kiwis were said to be calling in the forest at night. Maori people had settlements on both sides of the harbour, notably at Otakou (the site of a well-developed marae today), where there had been a busy whaling station in the 1830s. The Maoris traded

10

The great stone-vaulted nave of St Paul's Cathedral in the Octagon. The Gothic pillars, made of Oamaru stone, are over 40 metres high.

Straight as cathedral columns, 70-year- old Douglas fir tower above a garden of native astelia lilies in Flagstaff Forest.

Communal macrocarpa: Groves of the American conifer *Cupressus macrocarpa*, planted last century, are a feature of the Otago Peninsula landscape.

Tree-lined Logan Park Drive. The American poplars at left are wearing spring foliage.

with the settlers and canoed to the head of the harbour. The canoe landing was at what is now the southern end of Princes Street. The extensive tracts of tall forest have gone — and so have the kiwis — but significant remnants, especially on Otago Peninsula, enjoy protection.

Behold the noble city towering high
Above the silver mirror framed in green!

Thomas Bracken,
"James Macandrew" 1890

The discovery of gold in Central Otago in 1861 transformed Dunedin. No longer was it a backwater settlement dependent on farming for its future prospects. The gold rush triggered boom times. Requiring a larger port area, Dunedin expanded on to land reclaimed from the tidal flats. It grew to be not only the commercial capital of New Zealand, but also the largest main centre and the most influential. By 1874 Dunedin's population was 18,500 — a third bigger than Auckland's.

Dunedin's great stock of Victorian buildings is evidence of this 19th century surge in fortunes — the elegant old banks, hotels, public facilities, commercial buildings and residences. All manner of materials went into their construction — stone, brick, timber, concrete and plaster. In some cases, the developers imported architects, stonemasons and other talent to undertake the work. They were people of wealth and status, these developers, and they insisted on the very best.

Unlike Wellington and Auckland, which lost much of their built heritage to property

speculation and a sharemarket boom in the 1970s and 1980s, Dunedin retained a large number of its significant buildings. A few have been refurbished in recent times. Restoration of the Municipal Chambers in the Octagon — the original Town Hall — is symbolic of the renewed pride in the city in its historic buildings.

Fortunately, Dunedin missed out on the boom that produced canyons of sterile office blocks in the northern main centres. The high-rise label does not apply to Dunedin's downtown area. A sense of scale has been preserved; the spires and turrets still compete for attention on the central city skyline.

Monuments dotted about fortify the sense of history here, commemorating people and events. Pride of place goes to the legendary Scottish poet, Robert Burns. A bronze statue of Burns, who was the uncle of the co-leader of the Otago settlement, the Rev. Thomas Burns, overlooks the Octagon.

". . . a city built in stone on half a century of gold
from the hinterland, a wealthy little city where
the rich inhabited the hills and looked out to sea
and the poor inhabited the flat and looked at
each other."

Christine Johnston
"Blessed Art Thou Amongst Women" 1991

Dunedin is a literary city, claiming to have fostered many of New Zealand's distinguished writers, so it is fitting the pre-eminent statue should commemorate a writer. Embedded in the footpaths of the Octagon are a series of bronze

13

plaques that immortalise pithy comments about the city from significant writers down the decades (some of these quotations in this "Writers' Walk" are reproduced on these pages). The literary links are reinforced every second year by way of New Zealand Writers' Week, a Dunedin initiative that attracts an array of established and budding wordsmiths for a week of public functions, panel discussions, book launchings and readings.

Dunedin excels at theme weeks and festivals. The Dunedin Festival in February is a pageant of cultural and sporting activity and general good fun; Scottish Week in March celebrates the city's origins; a Food and Wine Festival the same month adds spice to city life; Rhododendron Week in October is promoted internationally; and a flurry of folk music sees in the New Year. The New Zealand Masters Games is a biennial event.

Dunedin's cultural milieu is highly developed. A city twice the size would be proud of its facilities and cultural calendar.

Performing arts are well served by professional theatre, operatic organisations, an orchestra, choirs, a folk club and an assortment of pub bands, some of which go on to win national fame. Collectively, the pub bands are known as the "Dunedin Sound".

Otago Museum and the Otago Early Settlers' Museum do a magnificent job of evoking the past, and the Dunedin Public Art Gallery has an inspiring collection of masterpieces. Library services are superb. For specialists, the University's Hocken Library and the Dunedin Public Library's McNab Room are treasure houses of published works, containing just about anything ever published on Dunedin and Otago.

As university lecturer and author, Austin Mitchell, noted in 1963: "Dunedin could well have . . . more music, theatre, culture, library books and pop singers per capita than most of the Dominion."

Outdoor recreation reflects the city's diverse physical setting — an all-rounder's playground.

"If climbing the hills be conducive to hardiness in a people, the citizens of Dunedin should excel in that quality, for one can hardly go anywhere without ascending an incline."

Alexander Bathgate
"Colonial Experiences" 1874

Morris Dancers celebrate May Day in an autumn-tinged Chingford Park.

Left:
The annual foot race on the world's steepest street — Baldwin Street, North-East Valley. The gradient, 1 in 2.9, is breathtaking.

The blooms of *Rhododendron giganteum* are impressively large (as the tree's name suggests). Dunedin's climate suits the cultivation of several hundred species of rhododendron.

Activities range from sub-alpine mountain biking to beach volleyball and windsurfing. Catch a salmon in the harbour or a trout on a Taieri ripple. Run the world's steepest street (a Festival Week race). Fly a hang-glider from a towering Peninsula cliff.

Dunedin's extensive coastline, a contrast of sandy and rocky shores, tempts exploration. More than 20 beaches of creamy sand are accessible within half an hour's drive of the city centre, and no matter the wind direction, there is a sheltered beach somewhere.

A stroll on a Dunedin beach is a good way to contemplate New Zealand's oceanic nature and the fickle character of the climate in these latitudes – the "Roaring Forties" (Dunedin lies close to the latitude line of 46 degrees south, halfway between the Equator and the South Pole).

Between bouts of fine weather and warm north-westerlies, cold fronts bear down darkly from the south and south-west quarters. At other times, north-east winds whip in from open ocean, annoying gardeners in the harbour suburbs, and by late afternoon tossing great banks of cloud on to the mountains flanking the city – Mount Cargill, Flagstaff and Swampy Summit.

Dunedin's climate is described as temperate (11 degrees celsius mean temperature; annual rainfall about 800mm) – not too hot, not too cold. The latitude produces fairly distinct seasons compared to northern parts of New Zealand, although the summers can be frustratingly short or patchy. What impresses most visitors is the changeable nature of the weather. Some days it can feel as if several seasons are vying for control all at once, with temperatures swinging 10 degrees in an hour and clouds arriving from nowhere.

It didn't make a grand entrance and I nearly
missed it – tip-toeing up on me as it did
when it was half asleep and suddenly, they're there
before my eyes – white pointillist flakes

Hone Tuwhare
"Snowfall" 1982

The cloudiness is no doubt linked to the hilly terrain. On a day when it is dull in the city proper, there can be bright sunshine at Mosgiel or Karitane. Like the landscape, the cloudscape does have scenic value. Never the same, the cloud patterns over Dunedin can be breathtaking at times, a passing parade of shapes and textures. Their effect on the light is equally impressive. In autumn and spring, low sun angles conspire with the clouds to spotlight suburbs like Waverley or St Clair. Sometimes the whole city is cast in dappled light.

Climate influences wildlife – the marine wildlife in particular. Dunedin is renowned for its large and spectacular seabirds, notably royal albatrosses and yellow-eyed penguins, but also the shags (cormorants). Clearly the temperate climate suits them. But there is more to it than that. They breed here because there is a reliable supply of food in the surrounding seas.

The same may be said of the marine mammals — the seals, sealions and dolphins. The sea is to their taste.

The continental shelf is narrow off Otago Peninsula, giving the seabirds and seals access to deep water relatively close to their breeding grounds. As a bonus, submarine canyons extend dark fingers towards the land.

The whole arrangement is convenient from a human point of view, too. It makes the wildlife handy and accessible — penguins doing their daily trips to sea a few kilometres from the city centre, and an albatross colony inside city limits instead of on some far-flung sub-Antarctic island.

Dunedin people are tuning into the wildlife on their doorstep as never before, spurred on by the promotion of their city as a natural history centre, a place where the rare and special reside.

Things uniquely natural and strikingly architectural underpin the city's tourist appeal. But there is more. A tourist train trip through a gorge full of tunnels and viaducts; a haggis ceremony; a riot of rhododendron colour. The diversity of interest is expressed in the city's official promotional slogan, adopted in 1988: **"Dunedin. It's all right here."**

Once reticent and not a little apologetic about its abundance of old buildings (as if old meant staid and old-fashioned), and once blind to its wealth of wildlife, Dunedin has awoken to the value of the things around and within it. In a sense, the slogan expresses the pleasant surprise of that awakening.

Otago Harbour, 22km long, is divided into upper and lower parts by Portobello Peninsula and two islands, which mark the centre of the long-dormant Dunedin Volcano. Portobello and Broad Bay are at centre left; Port Chalmers and Sawyers Bay centre right. At the head of the harbour is the city centre. Otago Peninsula (left), once an island, is tied to the mainland by a low sandy isthmus or tombolo. Mount Cargill (680 metres) is at the centre extreme right of the picture, with the Taieri Plain and the Maungatua Range in the right distance.

– Perran Tonkin photo

North Dunedin. The University of Otago campus (centre) and Dunedin Hospital complex (centre left) stand out. Beyond is the Town Belt bush and the suburb of Maori Hill, with Flagstaff overlooking all.

University students negotiate the quadrangle between lectures.

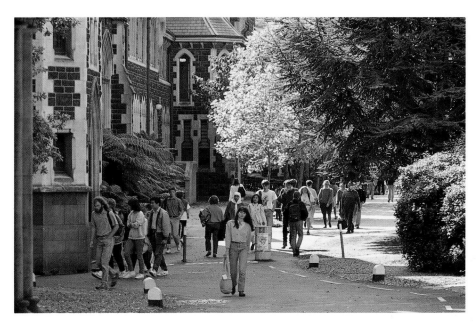

The campus, surrounded by a residential area, is a mixture of elegant old stone buildings and modern new concrete ones. Among the newer blocks are the brown-roofed Commerce Building and, to the right of it, the Hocken Building.

Otago Polytechnic occupies a new complex adjacent to the University.

Spring brings brilliant colour to the rock garden in the Dunedin Botanic Gardens.

The bronze statue of Peter Pan, Lower Gardens.

Right: A daffodil admirer in the Upper Gardens.

Winter in the Upper Gardens. Maple, azalea and magnolia trees stand bare above an understorey that features native ferns and lilies.

Above:

On a shoulder of Flagstaff lie the suburbs of Halfway Bush (left) and Wakari. At centre is Wakari Hospital.

Left:

The plateau inland of Flagstaff, called Swampy, is an expanse of tussock grasslands, subalpine herb fields and wet areas. On the high points there are telecommunications and aircraft navigation installations.

Right:

First to greet the summer sun — the suburbs of Roslyn, Maori Hill and, in the distance, Pine Hill.

Surf meets sandstone at Tunnel Beach.

St Clair is both beach and suburb. The Forbury Park circuit, for harness horse racing, makes a splash of green close to the sand. Near the rocky point is a swimming pool of heated sea water.

Surf rafting off St Clair Beach.

Volcanic headlands dominate the coastal scenery of Dunedin. Lawyers Head encloses Tomahawk Beach and beyond are the St Clair headlands and Black Head in the distance.

Mural on the St Clair Surf Lifesaving Club's headquarters.

The sands of Aramoana, with Taiaroa Head, form the entrance of Otago Harbour. Just beyond the village is a saltmarsh of major conservation interest. Otago Peninsula is in the distance.

Not the Grand Canyon, but knee-high sand "cliffs" sculpted by a small stream at Sandfly Bay.

Sunset colours a gentle surf at Aramoana.

Southerly storm brewing
over Otago Harbour.
Taiaroa Head is silhouetted
in a sunbeam.

Portobello Marine Laboratory, on Portobello Peninsula, is one of New Zealand's leading marine research institutions. With origins going back to 1904, it is administered by the University of Otago and has an aquarium open to the public. Opposite the complex is St Martin's (Quarantine) Island, originally known as Kamautaurua, which is owned by the Department of Conservation and leased to an interdenominational community.

Port Chalmers, halfway along Otago Harbour, is Dunedin's deep-water port.

Sandfly Bay is a wildlife refuge. There is a public yellow-eyed penguin viewing hide in the dunes at left. The prominent islet is known locally as Lion's Head.

Wintry scene on Otago Peninsula, with snow in the wind. In the distance, Hoopers and Papanui Inlets are glimpsed.

Portobello and Harbour Cone.

Overleaf: Lovers Leap, one of Otago Peninsula's top scenic attractions, is a collapsed sea cavern. There is a narrow rock bridge on the seaward side. Nearer the point is another collapsed cave — The Chasm. In the distance is Allan's Beach, enclosing Hoopers Inlet.

The bridal party arrives for a wedding at Larnach Castle.

Larnach Castle stands on a hilltop overlooking harbour and sea. The stone castle, completed in 1887, was the home of a banker politician, William Larnach. Its 34 rooms cover almost 4000 square metres. Open to the public, Larnach Castle has become a symbol of Dunedin's reverence for historic buildings.

Garden figure and ballroom, Larnach Castle.

Black Head, a volcanic headland south of the city, has spectacular formations of columnar basalt rock. Quarrying operations are slowly disposing of the bulk of the headland, although its outer end, featuring formations known as the Roman Baths and The Dock, is protected under a conservation covenant. In recent years, conservationists have campaigned to save all of the cliff faces.

Right:

The sun sets on a quiet surf at Black Head Beach. Green Island is in the distance.

Above:
Saturday afternoon sport – cricket on Logan Park; board sailors on the harbour.

Left:
Fly-fishing practice, Logan Park.

Competition day for marching teams, University Oval.

Saddle Hill, named by Captain Cook on his 1770 exploration, overlooks Mosgiel, the Taieri Plain's main centre. At centre is the Mosgiel Woollen Mills. New Zealand's first woollen cloth was manufactured here in 1871.

One of the Taieri's leading industries is the whiteware manufacturing plant owned by Fisher & Paykel on the site of the old Taieri aerodrome, a few kilometres from Mosgiel.

Billow cloud, the flag of strong north-west winds, stacks up over Saddle Hill and the Taieri Plain. Part of Flagstaff Forest is in the foreground.

A tourist train regularly plies the Taieri Gorge railway. Here the train approaches a tunnel before the bridge over the Taieri River.

A rafting party enjoys a barbecue lunch in the Taieri Gorge.

Left: Sheepwash Creek near Middlemarch, close to the eastern boundary of the City of Dunedin. Smooth Cone and its lone pine tree stand guard.

Snowbound: Winter scene at The Crater, a volcanic formation on Taieri Ridge, overlooking the Strath Taieri Valley. The tree is a kowhai.

Lower Taieri: Dunedin's main farming and market garden area.

Tawny tussock grasslands in the Silver Peaks Range.

The slowly expanding edge of a patch of native silver beech, known as the Painted Forest, in the Silver Peaks Range.

Overleaf: The Leith Valley winds beneath Ross Reservoir, a water supply for the city.

Purakanui Inlet, north of the city. The small promontory at centre, called Mapoutahi, was a defensive position for early Maori. In the distance is Warrington.

Port Chalmers. A motor vehicle transport vessel is berthed at the container wharf. Major wharf development is planned for the log berth opposite, by Observation Point.

The shape of things to come? A large-scale model depicts a scenario for development of the Dunedin waterfront. It features a reclaimed lagoon, dissected by the main trunk railway.

A pair of newly banded yellow-eyed penguin chicks at their Otago Peninsula nest site.

Nature's Sensations

PETER HAYDEN

When is the best time to see Dunedin's wildlife and enjoy the best of its natural features? That's a difficult question, but I'll do my best to answer it.

Perhaps **autumn** is best. It's the season when parks, gardens and the Town Belt blaze in the red and gold leaves of oak, elm, plane and sycamore trees, signalling the passion the settlers from Britain had to recreate another Europe. In the elegant evergreen Woodhaugh Gardens, however, there remains some of the city's original forest cover. Tall rimu, pokaka and kahikatea stand beside younger planted specimens. Indeed, that's the true 'nature' of Dunedin — a blend of old and not so old, of what has lived on the flanks of the ancient volcano long before humankind discovered the sheltered harbour and what we (mainly Europeans) transplanted here.

Far out at sea off Otago Peninsula, autumn is marked by days when, from horizon to horizon, thousands of muttonbirds (sooty shearwaters or titi) begin their migration to the northern Pacific from southern parts of New Zealand. It is a season, too, when tussocks ripple and bull kelp swirls at the approach of the first of the winter storms.

Winter is also a wonderful season in Dunedin. It is very dramatic, with sparkling clear days to contrast with the southerly fronts that lower the temperatures and drain colour from the landscape. It's a time when a walk in the hills can either be warm and refreshing or a test of survival skills. A snow storm can suddenly cloak Flagstaff and Mount Cargill, making their slopes fit for tobogganing.

On harbour shores kingfishers join little shags on the power lines, while inland cattle egrets and an occasional white heron are to be seen on farms. Rural ducks crowd the Botanic Gardens ponds, preferring death from an excess of bread and crusts to death from shotgun pellets. At Taiaroa Head, albatross chicks hatched in December are only now beginning to lose their baby feathers. They are moving about the colony socialising. But you'll be lucky to see them being fed. As winter gives way to spring,

parental diligence wanes.

In **spring** there's much to see in and around Dunedin. Far from their Asian homes, rhododendrons and azaleas bloom spectacularly and abundantly in the Botanic Gardens and in private gardens. They find much favour in the cool coastal climate. So do penguins. Spring is the time when two penguin species are hard at work tending eggs at the nest. The little blues come and go quietly from coastal caves and burrows, while the larger and rarer yellow-eyed penguins nest under flax or whatever coastal vegetation they can find. It's a pleasure to see these birds so close to the city. Much effort has been made to protect and enhance their nesting prospects.

At Taiaroa Head, last year's albatross chicks fly away to sea (they won't come back to the colony for four or five years) and the new season's adult birds arrive. They court, mate and lay eggs away from our curious eyes as the colony is closed to the public during this time.

But the journey to Taiaroa Head is not without rewards. Shags of two kinds can be seen in breeding plumage around the cliffs at the head of the Peninsula. There are seals to observe lazing or frolicking. Perhaps a southern right whale or humpbacked whale will swim in through the Heads. They are safe now; Dunedin's shore whaling station closed more than 100 years ago.

And do not forget **summer.** The weather may be capricious, but the hugely long day lengths allow for adventure and exploration on a grand scale. Out on the Peninsula, sea fogs that gently roll over the hills are harbingers of fine weather, and inland it's more than likely conditions will be searingly hot. Along the roadsides to and beyond Middlemarch, wild flowers bloom in the heat and dry.

Nature's year comes together in summer. Everything looks its best, and the next generation of wildlife is being cared for in many different ways and in many different settings.

So the answer as to when is the best time to get out and enjoy the natural sensations of Dunedin must be now . . . and always.

Above:

Harbour sentinel: Taiaroa Head, known also as Pukekura. The lighthouse buildings and signal station have red roofs; the visitor centre is at left.

Taiaroa Head is an extraordinary place for marine wildlife. The royal albatross colony, comprising about 100 birds, dates from 1938 when the first chick flew. The headland is also home to three species of shag or cormorant (Stewart Island, spotted and little) and a relatively large number of blue penguins. Red-billed and black-backed gulls also breed here, and there is a sooty shearwater colony in the vicinity.

Right:

A nesting pair of royal albatrosses with their chick. At breeding time the adult birds have reddish bills. From the tubes on the bill they drain excess salt.

Albatrosses spend more than 80 percent of their lives at sea.   — *Rod Morris photo*

Left:
Built for gliding, royal albatrosses have wingspans of up to three metres.
— *Greg Gordon photo*

Hands-on wildlife management work requires a great deal of dedication and commitment, and Dunedin has produced many such people over the years. Lance Richdale was a pioneer in the field, taking steps to protect the Taiaroa Head albatrosses from recurring vandalism. On these pages are some of the people who have devoted decades to wildlife management and research and helped make the Dunedin area more of a haven for wildlife.

Above:

"Grandma", a Taiaroa Head albatross who was still breeding at 60 years of age, allows her chick to be weighed by Shirley Webb, a member of the Department of Conservation team managing the colony.

Below:

A downy yellow-eyed penguin chick is banded by John Darby, who has kept records of Otago Peninsula birds since 1980.

Hooker's sea lions, whose breeding headquarters are the sub-Antarctic Auckland Islands, are making a comeback on mainland New Zealand. Otago Peninsula is a stronghold, although numbers are still small. Chris Lalas has studied the diet of these magnificent marine mammals.

A Hooker's sea lion on Victory Beach.

Above:

Green Island, off Kaikorai Estuary, is alive with seabirds. It holds breeding populations of yellow-eyed and blue penguins, Stewart Island and little shags, sooty shearwaters, fairy prions, variable (black) oystercatchers and, notably, royal spoonbills. The white dots in the bush are roosting spoonbills, which use Kaikorai Estuary (in the distance) as a feeding ground. The vegetation on the 300m-wide island is dominated by a small tree, taupata *(Coprosma repens)*. **Note:** Green Island is a nature reserve and closed to the public. Landings are not permitted.

Left:

First-born: A royal spoonbill chick, Green Island. Even at this early age, the chick displays the distinctive wide-ended beak for which its species is named. Juvenile or adult spoonbills feed by sifting mud or sand on tidal flats and sweeping their beaks from side to side.   *– Steve Broni photo*

54

Blue penguin, Aramoana.

Spotted shag colony, Taiaroa Head.

New Zealand fur seals are common on rocky parts of the Otago Peninsula coastline. Most are male, like this one. Breeding has become established in a few places.

Basking fur seal, Pilot's Beach.

Leith Saddle, high point on the Northern Motorway, contains showpiece stands of native forest featuring large rimu, matai and kaikawaka (cedar). This view is of the saddle area from above the treeline, looking towards Mount Cargill. The olive green foliage between the tussock shrublands and the forest edge is inaka or grass tree *(Dracophyllum longifolium)*.

New Zealand's only endemic daytime bird of prey, the New Zealand falcon, may be seen occasionally in the hills above the city. This bird is on Swampy Spur.

Native cedars, Leith Saddle.

An Otago skink basking next to a porcupine shrub.

Beyond the Dunedin Volcano, the geology is predominantly schist — an ancient sedimentary rock, prone to splitting and weathering. The Dunedin hinterland contains a large area of schist hill country, dramatically different landscape from that around Otago Harbour. Here is the home of spectacular lizards that live on schist outcrops or tors — the Otago skink and grand skink, largest of all mainland lizards, attaining a length of up to 28cm.

Left:
Crevices in the schist rock provide a home and hiding place for the Otago skink between periods of sunbathing and feeding.

A common copper butterfly in native wheatgrass, Sutton Salt Lake Scenic Reserve.

Below:
A picnic at Sutton Salt Lake, deep in Strath Taieri schist country. Lake levels vary from half a metre (full) to bone dry. Protected within a scenic reserve, this is New Zealand's only salt lake.

At the south end of the Taieri Plain are two shallow lakes — Waihola and Waipori — and a linking mosaic of channels, pools, islands, swamps and levees. Covering about 2000ha, they represent a wetland area that is vitally important for wildlife, especially waterfowl. Some uncommon or endangered birds live here, including Australasian bittern, banded rail, marsh crake and South Island fern bird. Eighty bird species have been sighted, 55 of them native. The wetland supports more than 10,000 ducks, and swans also live here.

Left:

Lake Waihola and wetlands linking it with Lake Waipori.

Black swans.

Old lava flows are reflected in this view over Victory Beach on Otago Peninsula, which is protected for nature conservation reasons. Yellow-eyed penguins nest in the remnants of low coastal forest. In the foreground is a line of kotukutuku or tree fuchsia, one of New Zealand's few native deciduous trees.

Left:
These yellow-eyed penguin chicks are almost ready to fledge.

Facing page: Dripping wet in late afternoon light, this adult yellow-eyed penguin has just returned from a day's fishing. This penguin species is unlike most others in that the birds remain at their breeding grounds throughout their adult lives and feed in local waters. They are relatively private penguins, choosing to nest out of sight of each other.

— *Dean Schneider photo*

Tree fern, Dunedin Botanic Gardens.

Full bloom: Clouds of honey-scented flowers on a native tree daisy, *Olearia aborescens,* at Sandymount Reserve, Otago Peninsula.

Eye-catching, educational and evergreen: The New Zealand Section in the Dunedin Botanic Gardens. From large indigenous conifers to colourful alpine cushion plants, the New Zealand Section boasts just about every shade of green going in nature. And there is always something in flower. Trees, shrubs, herbs, grasses and ferns from throughout New Zealand are displayed here.

Facing page: Summer on the Waipori River, with native mistletoe adding a splash of colour.

Right:
A silvereye or tauhou feasts on the nectar of native kowhai flowers — a portent of spring.

Below:
Kotukutuku *(Fuchsia exorticata)* freely sheds its bark, although not always as colourfully as this. This native tree, the world's largest fuchsia, is common in wet or shady areas around Dunedin. Its berries, konini, are delicious.

Character tree, the product of wind-shear, in an exposed Peninsula paddock.

Bull kelp *(Durvillaea antarctica),* common on the Otago coast, is one of the world's great seaweeds.
Stout holdfasts anchor the swirling leaves.

Stewart Island shags nest on mud-hardened pedestals at Taiaroa Head. This colony is one of the most
important for the species, which is confined to southern New Zealand.

The 12ha woodland garden of Glenfalloch has entertained visitors for decades with a mixture of introduced and indigenous plants. *Rhododendron giganteum* produces huge clusters of bell-like flowers in winter.

Otago Museum conveys a wealth of
information on the wildlife of Dunedin,
past and present. Bird collections include species
of albatross, penguin and shag (cormorant).
Insect life is portrayed in a series of different
habitats in a special insect hall. Sharks and
other marine creatures are also on display.
Towering moa and long-billed huia are among
the extinct birds exhibited.

The bronze statue of Scottish poet Robert Burns (1759-96), erected in the Octagon in 1877, symbolises Dunedin's Scottish origins.

Built Heritage

LOIS GALER

When Dunedin's Scottish settlers created their Edinburgh of the South last century, they also created what is regarded today as New Zealand's best preserved Victorian city. Here, the vandals of progress have made little impression. Compared to other New Zealand cities, the growth rate in Dunedin in the 20th century has been slow.

Though appearing far from the mainstream of industry and commerce today, Dunedin reflects an era when it led the country in these fields. This was before the turn of the century when the city was reaping the benefits of the gold discoveries in Central Otago. As both front and back door to this industry, as well as the first and last port of call for ships plying the Tasman, Dunedin became the main provider of everything from woollen goods to gold dredges.

These illustrious times before the gold ran out and the population began its gradual drift north were boom times. But if there was ever a hint that the boom would be short-lived, this is not reflected in the buildings the industrialists eventually left behind. "Build strong and to last" seems to have been the catchword — and last they did.

Typically for that period, businessmen tended to reflect their opulence in their buildings. And more than willing to help them achieve this were a number of young architects who had come to this new metropolis to test their skills with the many revival forms then fashionable worldwide. One of the best known of these was Robert Lawson, whose winning design for the First Presbyterian Church brought the young Scot from Melbourne in the mid-1860s. He stayed not only to supervise the church's construction, but to design such monuments to his name as the Municipal Chambers, Otago Boys' High School, the Union Bank (later the ANZ), Knox Church and a number of prestigious commercial buildings.

To satisfy the Scottish settlers' preference for stone buildings, Otago was able to yield plentiful supplies — hardy andesites from the Leith Valley, breccia from Port Chalmers and limestone from Oamaru. Good local clays were also turned into bricks. In Dunedin's heyday, as many as 40 brickworks are said to have operated at the same time. To create a stone appearance, brick buildings were generally plastered and grooved to resemble large blocks.

Another legacy from the Scots is Dunedin's fine educational institutions. When established in 1871, Otago University became the first university in New Zealand. This fine neo-Gothic complex of stone buildings in the city's north end pays tribute both to the city fathers and the architects who initially designed it then continued to add to the complex in the same design right up until the 1920s.

The same year the university was established, New Zealand's first State secondary school for girls — Otago Girls' High School — was founded. Both institutions went on to produce New Zealand's first practising woman doctor and the country's first woman barrister.

Opposite the girls' high school is another building of note, the former St Dominic's Priory. When built in 1877, it was the largest unreinforced concrete structure in the Southern

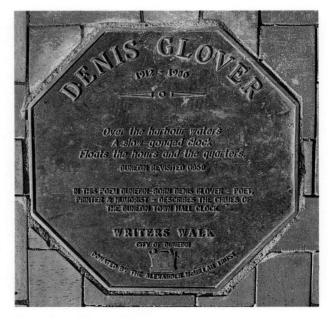

One of the Writers' Walk plaques, quoting poet Denis Glover.

Hemisphere. Its designer was one F. W. Petre, noted throughout the country for his basilica designs. His use of concrete for the priory and several well known Dunedin mansions earned him the title of 'Lord Concrete'!

Among the surviving industrial buildings is New Zealand's first major city gasworks — and the last to produce gas from coal, a function that lasted 124 years. With its boiler, chimney and engines intact, the complex is being developed as a coal, steam and gas museum.

Continuing to mill grain after 127 years is the Crown Roller Mill, a tall, brick Victorian edifice at the south end of the main street.

If head office buildings, banks and factories were designed with status in mind, so too were the homes of their owners and managers. Dotting the hill slopes above the city are some of the finest, including Olveston, designed by British architect Sir Ernest George just after the turn of the century and bequeathed to the city by the original owner's daughter in the 1960s.

Another notable residence, also open to the public, is Larnach Castle on the Otago Peninsula. 'The Camp', as it was called, was built in the 1870s for the Chief Colonial Manager of the Bank of Otago, William Larnach. In terms of a residence befitting a man's status, Larnach went a little further than most.

Considering it has the largest concentration of 19th century buildings in New Zealand, Dunedin as a heritage centre cannot be equalled in the country. For this, it has much to thank its 19th century founders — and fate for keeping progress in the 20th century to a minimum necessary for survival, leaving the city's identity intact.

As the Edinburgh of the South, Dunedin can now look forward to the 21st century, poised to greet a new era of even greater appreciation than the city enjoys today.

Right: An academic icon, the clock tower and registry building of the University of Otago has long been symbolic of higher education in Dunedin. It was built of volcanic Leith Valley andesite in the late 1870s — the most impressive feature of an imposing complex of Gothic buildings.

The bridge over the Water of Leith is perhaps the busiest part of the campus. The Archway building behind holds significance — traditionally the place where examination results are posted.

Above:

These tall semi-detached houses accommodated the University's first professors in 1879. They are named after the professors — Scott, Black, Sale and Shand. The Moeraki gravel roughcast was applied to the original dark red brick exterior in 1957. Today the houses are used as offices for several departments of the University, including the Extension Department.

Right:

University buildings and residential accommodation form a snug precinct.

Olveston, Dunedin's showpiece historic home, was designed by London architect Sir Ernest George and built between 1904 and 1906. It reflects Jacobean-style grace and grandeur. The 35-room home was built for David Theomin, a successful English-born importer and businssman, who had a passion for collecting. He and his family travelled extensively and lavished their home with irreplaceable artefacts and other treasures. Olveston was gifted to the city, complete with its original contents, by the late Miss Dorothy Theomin in 1966. Opened to the public in October 1967, Olveston is one of Dunedin's finest attractions.

Right:

An acre of trees, lawns and gardens surrounds Olveston. Moeraki pebbles and Oamaru stone facings colour the exterior of the house.

Below:

Olveston's grand hall. The oak staircase, erected without the use of nails, was shipped out from Britain.

The drawing room.

Dunedin Railway Station, New Zealand's finest railway edifice, was opened in 1906. It is built of Kokonga basalt, a volcanic stone, with Oamaru stone facings.

The Railway Station's main foyer is decorated with shiny majolica tiles. Over 700,000 squares of Royal Doulton porcelain make up the mosaic floor.

Ticket booths in the main foyer of the Dunedin Railway Station. With the demise of suburban passenger services, they are no longer in use.

A relic of the age of steam, this JA locomotive has been retired to a glass case where it is on public display. It ceased service in 1971.

Above:

Otakou Marae near Taiaroa Head (Pukekura) is a major focal point for Maoridom in Dunedin. These gates, the church behind and the meeting house of Tamatea commemorate the centenary of the 1840 signing of the Treaty of Waitangi.

Left:

The marae is a complex of meeting house, church, cemetery and a block containing a dining room, kitchen, runanga office and kohanga reo classroom for pre-schoolers.

First Presbyterian Church of Otago — commonly called First Church — was opened in Moray Place in November 1873 after six years' construction. It was the third church on the site, the predecessors being small wooden buildings. The spire is 54 metres high.

Stained glass window in St Barnabas Church, Warrington.

Chingford Stables, set in a woodland park in North-East Valley, were built of Leith Valley bluestone (andesite) in 1880 for the Arab stallions of a prominent Dunedin businessman. Today the renovated stables are used for public functions.

Right:
A tile mural depicting yellow-eyed penguins decorates a corner of the Octagon.

Left:
Gothic Revival: St Paul's Cathedral in the Octagon is the seat of Anglican worship in Dunedin. It was built of Oamaru stone over a four-year period and consecrated in 1919.

Above:

A rock called Rongo from the Taranaki coast, installed near Andersons Bay Inlet, commemorates the suffering and deaths of Maori prisoners who were brought to Dunedin in the 1870s and 1880s as a result of the North Island land wars. The prisoners helped build the causeway across the inlet.

Left:

This earnest-looking bronze figure represents "History" at the Centennial Memorial on Signal Hill, a spectacular lookout. The memorial was erected in 1940 to commemorate the signing of the Treaty of Waitangi 100 years earlier. A piece of rock from Edinburgh Castle is embedded in the lookout.

Otago Boys' High School, next to the Town Belt, has a roll of about 900. It was opened in August 1863, but the ornate stone tower block was not erected until 1884.

These stone buildings near the Water of Leith house New Zealand's only existing whisky distillery, which launched its brands in 1974. Beer was brewed in these premises last century.

Lime was burnt in these Peninsula kilns last century for fertiliser and construction use. The kilns date from 1865.

Above:

Architectural landmark: The construction of Larnach Castle was supervised by architect Robert Lawson, who has left his mark in the heritage landscape of Dunedin. A Scot, Lawson came to Dunedin from the Victorian goldfields in the 1860s. He designed the Municipal Chambers and Otago Boys' High School, but he specialised in churches. First Church and Knox Church were among his achievements.

Left:

The kauri homestead of George Gray Russell adds a stately air to Glenfalloch's woodland garden. Russell lived on the site in 1860. The homestead serves teas and meals and has been hired out for functions for many years.

The Dunedin Town Hall, opened in 1930, has a huge main auditorium, with seating for over 2000 people. Profits from the South Seas Exhibition held in the city in 1925-26 stimulated its design and construction.

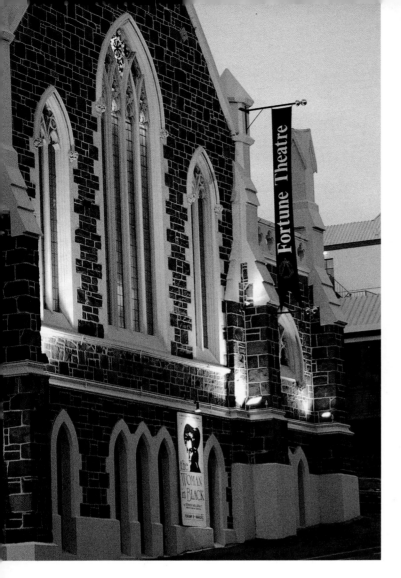

"Justice" — a figure on the Law Courts building in Lower Stuart Street.

Left:

Since 1978, Dunedin's professional theatre, the Fortune, has occupied an old stone building, the former Trinity Methodist Church, on the corner of Moray Place and Upper Stuart Street. The main auditorium seats about 240.

Ornamental detail on the former New Zealand Insurance building in Crawford Street.

The rusting remains of the trawler *Hananui II* are exposed at low tide on Ryans Beach, Otago Peninsula. The vessel went ashore in fog in 1943.

Historic graveyard: Young and old lie buried on St Martin's Island, which was a quarantine station from 1863 until the early 1920s. The headstone commemorates the first keeper of Quarantine Island, John Dougall.